7 BASICS TO BE A CHILD AGAIN

A NEW-AGE PARENTING GUIDE

CHANDRA KUMARI M

TO

CHERITH

PRERITH

ANAISHA

Contents

Acknowledgements

I cannot express enough gratitude to *The ALMIGHTY* for making all of this possible. *GODDESS SARASWATI* has been kind to me. *SHANTI GURUDEV* has been generous.

I also thank the ones who are The Almighty personified – *MAA* and *PAPA* for your blessings.

I extend heartfelt thanks to my sisters *SANTOSH, BHAVNA* and *DIMPLE* for the words of encouragement and the unhindered trust you have in me. You have been instrumental in my progress.

I thank *CHETAN* for being a constructive critic and always enlightening me on areas of improvement. Your suggestions inspire me and compel me to strive and achieve more.

I thank my husband, *HEMANTH*, who believed in the dreams of his homemaker wife. He never drew boundaries around me and trusted I was capable of more. From reading the drafts to giving helpful feedback, I am grateful to have you by my side.

Thank you, *JAY*, for the reviews and for self-appointing yourself, my editor.

I want to thank my best friends *MEENA, SWETHA* and *REEMA* for entering my life in the same order, giving me the space to express myself freely and staying with me for decades.

Thanks to my wonderful *COUSINS* for cheering me up, supporting me and keeping me updated.

I want to thank *EVERYONE* who has taught me something.

I thank *YOU*, my reader for picking this book up.

ONE
INTRODUCTION

"Every child born into the world is a new thought of God, an ever fresh and radiant possibility."- Kate Douglas Wiggin

ᕫᕫᕫ

Childhood serves as the foundation of every individual's personality, influencing the kind of adults and, eventually, parents we become. Our upbringing, the environment we grew up in, the kind of family and friends we have, and the adversities we face as children greatly influence our beliefs, practices, and how we navigate through life's challenges as adults.

In today's world, parents face numerous challenges related to their child's health, emotional and physical well-being, education, overall development, choice of sports, extracurricular activities, and mindful upbringing. We need to reflect on these challenges and look inward.

To be good parents to our children, we need to connect with our inner child and empathize and relate to our children. We need to be child first and a parent who simply asserts authority.

I share my experiences and lessons to help fellow parents on their journey. The anecdotes and examples intend to offer practical solutions to real problems. These have been pivotal in my parenting journey. I hope they prove instrumental in fostering deep and meaningful parent-child relationships and curating enriching experiences for ourselves and our children.

Let us embark on the journey of self-transformation together.

ᐧᐧᐧ

TWO

KEEN LEARNER

Active parenting starts the moment a child breathes for the first time. While mothers start with learning to handle and feed the baby, fathers often participate by helping the baby burp and changing the diapers.

We gradually learn how to keep track of our baby's needs, like the number of times our baby passes urine and how to understand our baby's cries. We seem to be on our toes even at subtle cooing or gurgling sounds our baby makes.

We learn to be patient during sleepless nights, illnesses, and the constant care they require. Keeping up with their vaccinations and ensuring they receive all the necessary doses becomes a significant part of our responsibilities. Parenting reveals the multitasker within us, and we become caregivers, protectors, and providers.

As our children grow, these roles take a backseat. Toddlers are a world of wonders, and I recall Sadhguru's words about how a child can turn a simple object into a universe. We grown-ups do that too, but we can a mountain out of small hurdles of life. I've realized that we tend to focus more on negative or challenging situations as adults, while children find joy and fascination in the simplest things.

ᑭᑭᑭ

One day, when my son was about a year and a half, I took him to one of his cousin's house. I sat there for a while believing he would want to come back with me. Instead, he settled on the floor creating sounds with a small glass and a spoon given to him. I stood at the door waving at him, calling his name for him to respond and he did not bother even looking at me. He played for two hours and was dropped back home when I started missing his presence.

There are so many times that his eyes and mind were focused on one particular thing at a time. He saw someone eating a chocolate, his gaze would be fixated there. When he found another kid playing with something, his ears would be turned off to all my callings. If we adults, could be so focused on the good things in life and mute the useless stuff around, wouldn't life be bliss??

I've learned so much from my child every day. For instance, he would have accidently hurt his head (as do many toddlers when they learn how to walk) and cry inconsolably but when I held him in my embrace, kiss him and lovingly stroked his hair, he would stop crying. A few loving words and a hug would make him forget any negative experience so easily. I learnt to forget and move on.

He would enter the kitchen and see a cucumber, tomato or banana and jump as if he's found a treasure. I learnt to cherish small things in life.

The sofa was nothing short of an adventure sport for him. He tried to climb it without caring if he'd make it or if he'd fall back. After relentlessly trying for a few days, he mastered ascending it. He taught me the value of persistence. If you work hard to get what you want you are sure of getting it someday. (Why worry which day?)

Whenever his favourite song played on TV, he sprang up to dance, moving his hands, feet and waist in an unsynchronised dance form. He played indoors all day but when he got to go out, it was nothing short of a festival! I learnt to live light-headed, celebrate little joys and become carefree. (Why bother about how you look?)

As he grew, I learnt from him that it's alright not to be available all the time, something which we as parents never practise. He continues to remind me to do what I like, treat myself, have fun, be fearless, get out of my comforts and do something unlike me and to live now, worry later.

ᐅᐅᐅ

My sister's son however, is cut from a different cloth. He is a peace-loving child and spends most of his time with his toys. With no other child to play with, I have seen him engrossed in creating something unique with his blocks, painting, and drawing. Once he is done, he is delighted to share his accomplishments with his mother and us through pictures and videos.

He is so focused while playing alone that he ends up creating robots with tiles, slides with wooden jenga blocks and vehicles with puzzle pieces. He can checkmate while playing snakes and ladders. Unique as it may sound, it gives me immense joy to see the creations of his artistic vision.

Observing my sister's son, I've learned the importance of being content and happy in one's own company. His ability to create and engage himself in play without needing constant external stimulation is a valuable lesson for us all. He demonstrates the significance of self-love and finding happiness within oneself.

ᑭᑭᑭ

Anaisha, my brother's daughter possesses a dangerously unique blend of my mother's and grandmother's genes. At times, she does behave like an old lady, but she never ceases to amaze us with the observations made by her skilful pair of eyes.

So when her mom tells her, it's not the correct way to talk. "It's wrong," stays with her. When she sees one of us do the same, she jumps in, "No, this is wrong. You should not do this!" Simply and directly, she forces us to *practise what we preach.*

Anaisha is an astute observer. She once looked at her mom going through daily chores without a break. She went to her mom, held her hand and made her sit down.

"Mumma," she enacted inhaling and exhaling deeply and continued slowly and softly, "Relax!"

That is such a small word but conveyed with so much precision. Isn't it what we as parents keep doing continually? We carry out tens of tasks outside and have hundreds of thoughts in our minds. It is indeed imperative for us to just take a break.

ᑭᑭᑭ

Isn't it amazing how children have such great clarity about themselves, about what they like and dislike? They can put across bluntly when they disagree. They express themselves freely. They do not care about being politically correct. They do not measure profits or losses while speaking their mind. Children love themselves, happy and comfortable the way they are before being introduced to feelings of doubt, shame, guilt and acceptance of the elder-world.

ᑭᑭᑭ

Likewise, teens have a distinctive vision of the world. That may not be the reason for all the clashes that parents have with teen children. Not being able to learn about their transition, to respect their space, to care without hovering above them all the time, to keep uncalled advice until asked for and to stop constant scrutiny of their actions are the real spoilers.

I'm sure of experiencing many more courses as I witness his evolution from a child to a teenager and finally advancing to becoming a handsome adult.

ᐅᐅᐅ

In summary, children teach us valuable lessons about resilience, joy, persistence, and self-contentment, and as parents, we can learn a lot from their innocent and carefree approach to life.

Let us keep the learning child in us awake, never letting it into a slumber to create an energetic and empathetic ambience for our children. Let us also learn the art of loving ourselves unconditionally before looking for love outside.

ᐅᐅᐅ

"The capacity to learn is a gift; the ability to learn is a skill; the willingness to learn is a choice."- Brian Herbert

ᐅᐅᐅ

THREE

TOO MUCH IN TOO LITTLE

Once, during his kindergarten days, my son, Cherith had a long weekend off from school from Friday to Sunday. I usually received details of home assignments through the mail. I was sceptically relieved that there was none despite the long weekend.

However, on Sunday night, I discovered that Cherith had six activity sheets to complete by Monday, and it felt like a bombshell at 11:30 at night. I could not leave it unfinished, so the three of us started working on it. I went through the activities while Cherith and my husband gathered the materials.

1. Paste pieces of orange crepe paper on the letter Q.
2. Colour pink on the pictures that start with R.
3. Sprinkle sand on the letter S.
4. Paste a picture of three objects that begin with the letter T.
5. Dab a balloon dipped in brown colour on the letter U.
6. Draw and colour an object that begins with W.

It seemed a task at that hour.

We started with W. The watermelon was done quickly. I drew it, my son coloured it, and my husband sat with a stack of newspapers looking for pictures with T. In another 5 minutes, that was done too.

I had crepe papers, but we did not have any orange to be used for Q.

"I'll do something." my husband said.

For the other letters, we neither had pink and brown water colours nor a balloon or sand. I hated to let Cherith go to school with unfinished homework.

Instantly, my husband pulled out white crepe paper and started colouring it orange. I looked at the box of watercolours. There were white, red, blue, green, black and yellow.

I looked up the internet to see what colours were to be mixed to make pink and brown.

Red + White = Pink. I got on to work, and quickly mixed the colours, the result achieved and R done.

Now for brown, equal amounts of red, blue and a little white if dark brown is needed. I started mixing the pink (red and white) with blue but got lavender.

It was midnight already and my son was looking at both of us busy with our make-shifting skills. After another 10 minutes, I could mix up and make something close to brown. We still did not have a balloon!

My husband dug into the box that had crepe papers and found a balloon lying underneath.

Cherith rejoiced, " We got it, Mom!"

So we finished U. For the Q, we used white crepe paper, coloured orange on one side.

My husband carefully cut it into pieces, and I and Cherith started pasting them. The letter Q was done.

"Where shall we get the sand from?" I asked

"We'll deal with S in the morning" he replied and we wound up everything and went to bed.

But Cherith was restless, "Mumma, let's do it now only. Please?"

I turned to my husband and saw him heading out to find sand. After 5 minutes he came back with some sand on a piece of paper. Finally, S done!! The three of us slept, my son was the happiest.

We were able to complete all the activities by improvising and working together. This experience made me realize the value of resourcefulness and creativity when faced with challenges.

I, and my husband did not have the luxury of variety in our childhoods, and Cherith got the opportunity to witness the fruit of the same. When provoked to work with too little, we become resourceful in creating way more than we think. It's an inbuilt trait in children who grow up in a middle-class environment.

ᐳᐳᐳ

That diverts my thoughts to the most successful people I have known and read about. From businessmen to sportspeople, from scientists to inventors, from teachers to artists, and from engineers to technicians, all of them have achieved great things when propelled to work with limited resources.

ᐳᐳᐳ

My father, for instance, came to Bangalore with merely 25 rupees. He spent 20 on the train ticket and 1 rupee on food during his journey from Rajasthan. He still takes pride in saving the 4 rupees.

He uses the soap until it sticks to his hand and refuses to lather. He uses the paste until the swollen tube is as flat as paper. He squeezes the bottle till the time he can see the last drop of oil in it. The essentials at home, his clothes, his footwear, the groceries and his children are well aware of his resourcefulness. It is visible in his way of life and has passed down to me and my family. It's a quality that I greatly value.

ᗅᗅᗅ

Irrespective of our social and financial standing, let us not overindulge our children as parents. Let us not underestimate the power of scarcity to push our children to think better and foster innovation. As a trait of a good child, we must exercise inventive ways to unfurl invaluable ingenuity in our children.

Necessity is the mother of invention. Lack of time and resources is for sure the Father of Innovation!!

ᗅᗅᗅ

"Man needs his difficulties because they are necessary to enjoy success."- APJ Abdul Kalam

ᗅᗅᗅ

FOUR

ACCEPTING BLUES AND PINKS

A celebration of buddies' day in Cherith's school required him to wear something pink during his Montessori days. After going through his wardrobe, I failed to find anything pink. So I decided to buy one.

Finding something pink turned out to be a task. The saleslady at the usual store I went to started picking different shirts from the rack.

"I need a pink shirt for my son," I said.

She immediately placed the shirts from her hand back on the rack and announced, "No madam, you will not get it."

I insisted her to check again, hoping to find at least one.

"We do not have anything pink for boys," she claimed.

After walking in and out of at least six to seven stores, going through heaps of kidswear and a good amount of people involved in the search mission, I managed to find a sole pink shirt.

I thought then, that this colour discrimination with clothes happens at the manufacturer level!!

Firstly, there are a few dressing options for boys (parents of male children will agree). Second, every store has a 70:30 ratio. The clothing stock for girls is higher than that for boys. The most annoying thing is the dedication of particular colours for boys' and girls' attire.

Girls have more options with red, pink, and orange, while boys' choices are limited to blues, greens and greys.

Although colours are universal, we assign boys blue and pink to girls even before birth. I can imagine the plight of the other colours. I understand they might be feeling out of place or feeling like dangling in-between as they would be looked at only when blues and pinks won't be available.

On a serious note, this colour discrimination results in shaming and teasing at young ages. Especially the boys wearing pink. I remember my husband's nephew had been bullied by his schoolmates for wearing a pink t-shirt. He came home and swore never to wear it because he had been called a girl for wearing pink.

ᐅᐅᐅ

Cherith once asked me if boys could wear pink.

"Yes. Why do you ask?"

"Mumma, brother says that is only for girls."

No matter what I told him later, he did not seem convinced.

ᐅᐅᐅ

We went out one day, and I found a man wearing a pink shirt. " Do you see that Uncle, Cherry?" I directed his eyes to the man looking the other way. "What colour is he wearing?" I asked

"Pink, mumma"

"Isn't it looking nice?" I asked further

"Very nice," he said and his face lit.

"We're surrounded by many colours. God has made all of them for each one of us. So, anyone is free to wear any colour." I concluded, watching him as he looked assured.

ᐅᐅᐅ

During my childhood, I was told that taking up a job, earning, late nights and night outs were only for boys, while cooking, cleaning, stitching, painting, and dancing were tasks solely for girls. As a result, I never had a chance to enjoy a slumber party and my brother was prohibited entry to the kitchen to learn how to make his favourite dish.

ᐅᐅᐅ

While watching a cricket match between India and the West Indies, a relative commented, "Look at those dark-skinned West Indians."

I looked at my son to see how he was taking that remark.

He replied, "All of us are creations of nature, and we are all beautiful in our way."

I was thankful that he remembered our conversations about the same. I told him, "We are all created by one creator, and he makes us all different because there is no fun in being the same. Each of us is blessed with talent, and we have our shortcomings. Making fun of people for the way they look is called body shaming. It means making fun of what God has created. That is not a good thing to do, is it?"

ᐅᐅᐅ

Another time, while watching a music reality show, someone laughed at a heavily built child. Though he was cute and had an exceptionally soulful voice, people judged him by his looks at first sight.

He repeated a few of my words, to their dismay. "We should not make fun of others because they are created by the same God that created us."

ppp

Unkind comments, brazen mentions and actions that normalize picking at someone for their appearance, accent, clothes or status not only intrigue but also crush the emotion of impartiality in children's blooming minds.

Let us accept the pinks, blues, and all the colours just like a child does. By this, I mean welcoming divergent backgrounds and a variety of ideas. I mean not designating or forbidding tasks based on gender. I mean not making fun of a fat or lean person, not remarking on skin colour. I mean not giving extra attention to someone rich and ignoring someone who is not. I mean not questioning religion and ethnicity. I mean giving due regard to personal choices.

Like a child, we need to accept the world, the way it is. Once we set out to do that, nothing would fuel discrimination that infuriates the fundamental rights of every human.

Perhaps then, a girl will not be looked down upon if she does not know how to cook, working late will not be a taboo, and helping in household chores will become common with male children.

ppp

Remember the times we played on the street with kids? None of the clothes, the skin colour, the backgrounds, and the status mattered, as long as we knew the names. Embracing inclusivity will lead to having all hues beautifully blended to make lives as stunning as a rainbow.

ᏜᏜᏜ

"Children are the living messages we send to a time we will not see."- John F. Kennedy

ᏜᏜᏜ

FIVE
QUESTIONS AND ANSWERS

From the moment you hold the baby in your arms, see them cuddle and fall asleep like it is the best place in the world, the journey is exhilarating.

In the first year, every month brings in some new visible changes in a child. In the following years, much more happens within the minds of the little menace makers in our lives.

My son has been swamping me with questions since he was 3. It was the time he started not just seeing but even observing.

He asked me questions like,

"Where do babies come from?"

"Why did you get married?"

"Why do you live with my papa and not with your mumma and papa?"

"Why is Earth the only place we people live in?"

"Why do we have to listen to elders all the time?"

"Why do we have to behave a certain way, when our elders do not behave the same way?"

ᐅᐅᐅ

His thoughts showered on me like war bombings without warning. Whilst I was glad about the questions, I tried my best to answer all of them in a simple manner, so he was satisfied with the answer and wouldn't consider going to anyone else for answers.

I still love this process of him doing internal brainstorming resulting in offbeat questions. I think it is a sign of a sharp mind. I must confess, however, that I asked a lot of questions too, as a child but barely got any answers.

Back then, I got one of these responses.

"Do it because you are told."

"That is how it has been."

"Our ancestors set traditions, and we follow them."

The best one was "Where do you get such strange thoughts?"

All of them sounded the same to me but none answered to my quizzical mind. The 'hungry for knowledge' child that existed in me helps me evaluate my child's questions more sensibly. I do not shoo away any of his questions regardless of whether they are awkward, unconventional, funny or curious.

ᐅᐅᐅ

Cherith, Prerith and Anaisha are 8, 6 and 3 respectively. These are the three little ones among me and my siblings. Their mini mouths bombard us with questions about God and ghosts, birth and death, love and loss, right and wrong, gender and body and anything that grasps their attention.

There is no particular place or time for these questions. They are thrown at us unannounced, and we're expected to answer them in a fashion acceptable to their unsettling minds.

In the process, we have learnt to admit if we do not have answers. We ask for some time to get a better understanding and revert. We try not to weigh them down with overwhelming replies. We try to use age-appropriate language. We do not want them to be further confused. We trust that we are doing a fairly decent job in maintaining a non-judgemental ambience. We're hopeful our children will continue to come to us with their questions at each stage of their lives.

"The way we talk to our children becomes their inner voice."-*Peggy O'Mara*

ᗞᗞᗞ

At one instance, my son spilt a little water while drinking from the glass. "Please wipe it off after you finish" I asserted.

I was preparing dinner. He replaced his glass, fetched the kitchen cloth and kneeled to wipe the floor. When his grandmother walked in, she teased, "Are you a housemaid to be cleaning the floor?"

He replied, "I spilt the water, so I'm wiping it off. I don't have to be a maid to clean my own house." without leaving room for rebuttal.

Another time, he was teased, "Are you a girl to roll out chapatis (flatbreads)?"

He replied, "Is it necessary for only girls to work in the kitchen? What is wrong with boys helping their mom?" diffusing the idea of further arguments.

ᗞᗞᗞ

To come to think of it, the child in me also has many questions. They may be a little complicated given the age and stage of life I am at, but they are unanswered nonetheless.

"Why are sweets circulated at the birth of only male children?"

"Why does the girl have to leave her house after marriage?"

"Why are daughters-in-law subject to continuous scrutiny when sons-in-law are accepted with open arms unopposed?"

"Why is it atypical for men to help their spouses?"

"Why is the money we own valued more than our qualities?"

"How can human lives have more value than animals?"

"Why do we keep damaging the environment when we can see its ill effects before our eyes?"

"What is the true measure of love?"

My list is unending. Despite the volcanic eruption of queries in my brain, I continue to ask them.

ܔܔܔ

As much as asking questions are important, answering them like a child holds its value.

I had recently kept a few old clothes aside to donate. My son picked one of those, and when I saw him in it, I blurted, "Why did you wear this t-shirt?"

"To cover my body," came his reply that overturned my exasperation to joyful humour.

One other time, when his friend had come home, I asked, "What did you have for dinner?"

"Khichdi," he replied referring to a dish made with lentils and rice.

"Why did you have khichdi for dinner?"

"Because my mother made khichdi for dinner."

I was bowled by the amusing simplicity that he reciprocated with. It reinstated that all situations need not require a microscopic lens. Relaxing or perhaps including innocence in our outlook may be just enough to appreciate life's gifts.

ϷϷϷ

Let the child in us also pursue the questions that come from within our hearts. It will aid exploration and better interpretation of the world.

The key is to have open conversations, including inconvenient ones, along with having a listening ear. It's the only way we can earn the trust which will remain unperturbed throughout. It is human to be incapable of knowing the solutions. It is alright as long as a channel to put them forth is intact. Answers can be sought together, but the absence of a trustworthy mode of communication can be devastating.

ϷϷϷ

"We should all be inspired by children: they don't care about fear and mistakes."- Maxime Lagacé

ϷϷϷ

SIX

CO - EQUAL

Who do we share our problems with? That sounds like a vague question. Allow me to rephrase it. Who do you see your children share their problems or interests with? It is usually other children, their friends or classmates.

Have you seen your child walk a little away while talking to a friend on the phone? Have you ever experienced a sudden silence in a room bustling with chatter and laughter right before you entered?

The reason is simple. The authority we display obstructs our children from speaking their minds after a certain age.

Children tend to share their interests, bizarre ideas, and imaginations with those they trust. They are confident that the person will not judge them for talking about impossible things and will not demotivate them to be grounded when they mention hundreds of thousands of figures.

They feel a sense of equality with such individuals. That equality encourages them to open up. Whether it is about their mother who reprimanded them or the praise they received in class, be it the stars, the universe, money, movies, cartoons, siblings or family, they boldly express the unfiltered ideas that spring to their minds.

ᗰᗰᗰ

I have heard many comparisons of childhoods using negative remarks about the present generation with one or more of the following lines.

- "You have all the facilities and privileges. We did not have any of these."
- "You get whatever you want. We had to wait for months before we got anything we asked for."
- "You make your own choices. We did what we were told."
- "We played inexpensive games, wore non-branded clothes and ate what was served without fuss."
- "The children of this generation are spoiled."

Such statements coming from parents further detach children from them, leading to constant arguments and disagreements. We should try taking the shoes of a parent off and stepping into our child's shoes.

More often than not, the problem is not the problem in itself. The barrier between a parent and the child is the problem. This barrier can be overcome by sharing. A child's mischief, anger, and tantrums all have a reason, which is usually not visible until we look at it from a child's perspective.

Furthermore, sharing strengthens bonds unimaginably. Sharing parts of our lives with our children opens them up to share their stories without feeling forced.

Make them feel it's okay to make mistakes and that their effort to rectify the damage is appreciated. Confessing is respected. Being truthful is applauded. Maintaining discipline is crucial. Building trust is very crucial. We would want our children to come to us with problems than go to others.

Deficiency of attention is one aspect that creates a feeling of inequality. Spending time with the child, using alone time without gadgets, playing games together, taking a walk, or simply noticing minute changes in their behaviour all convey that we are paying attention.

Research proves that lack of attention affects the psychological and mental progress of a child. We are required to place ourselves on the same level rather than expecting children to act subserviently.

I would like to highlight the presence of grandparents here. Their influence on a child's mind is immeasurably indispensable.

My mother-in-law is less authoritative while dealing with my son. Her understanding nature allows him to explain the reasons for his behaviour. He goes to her when he feels his mother will not empathize. Her jovial mannerism makes him forget his exasperation sooner.

Once, he stormed in angrily after a game with his playmates and complained about how one of them had hurt his leg. My mother-in-law replied, "So your leg is hurting?"

"Yes," he screamed fuming.

"Shall we order a new one on Amazon then?" she laughed.

My son's anger doused. He smiled from under his simmering exterior.

Sometimes, they play ludo and carrom on the phone and solve word puzzles and crosswords. She walks on the street when he goes out cycling or spends time with him on the terrace looking at aeroplanes that land at the nearby airport. They equally enjoy the rain and laugh until their stomachs ache watching comedy shows.

$\wp\wp\wp$

Fathers, on the other hand, usually do not get to spend too much time with their offspring. Needless to say, they do not do it out of choice. Their responsibility towards their families compels them to. We may feel that our child doesn't notice, but they do.

Once, I set up a competition between my son and my husband to create something unique with building blocks while I finished my routine. When I returned, I saw a robot and a railway bridge stacked next to each other.

"Which one is better?" my son asked.

I pointed to the one on my right and he clapped in jubilation.

"Did you make it?" I asked pretentiously.

"Yes!" he exclaimed

"It's wonderful! Now tell me what you want as a gift for making this amazing robot?"

"I do not want any gift mumma, I only want Papa to play with me for some time"

His naïve remark highlighted the deficiency of attention from his father and he confessed to me a few times that he wished he gets more time with his father.

A short trip planned immediately after gave him the assurance that he means so much more to his parents and we try to reinforce that feeling as and when possible. On that outing, he spent time swimming with his father, playing badminton with me, listening to music with us, relishing great food and capturing memories in hundreds of pictures. We were most elated to see him cheerfully enjoying all of it with his parents who did not behave like parents.

Thus, we need to be that child in their lives before behaving like a know-it-all parent. We need to look at things in the way they do to give them the security of being treated as equals.

As Dr. Seuss quotes –

"A person's a person, no matter how small."

ᕤᕤᕤ

Violence is another factor we need to look at. It can happen in many forms but I would like to closely consider the violence that a child is subject to at home. Many a time parents resort to hitting a child when he/she would behave inappropriately. I confess to landing a slap on my son's back a few times in the past.

Unaware of its consequences on the delicate mind of a child at the time, I believed it to be the only way to keep his temper in check. Here, I was paying no attention to my temper. Eventually, I started feeling there was no need for it because if I communicated my thoughts by going down to his level, there were very less chances he would not understand.

On his 5th birthday, along with his presents, I apologized to him for treating him roughly in the previous years. I promised him never to resort to any form of violence. I was appalled by my behaviour but I could not go back and change it. Although I have, since then only spoken to him about my thoughts and I was bewildered to see he listened.

I reckon he once surprisingly remarked, "How have you changed, mumma?"

"Have I?" I tried to make sense of what he was trying to say

"Yes, and so much. You listen to me and even when I am sure you will scold me for what I did, you only tell me what I can do better and that's it! You don't behave like before, angry and shouting." There was a sense of safety in his manner of confiding in me.

I don't find him shutting his eyes before I react to any of his blunders. He is not feared to share his mistakes anymore.

ᚦᚦᚦ

Do we ever see what violence does? When we raise our hand to hit our child, we are mentally putting ourselves in a position higher than that of a child, which automatically lays the foundation of inequality. Even the children who witness violence at home display unlikely behaviours. These actions have lasting effects on children.

On the other hand, if we discover that our child has been a part of a violent recourse, we only need to talk to them patiently and know the cause. Violence will either lead to a submissive child or an even more violent child, both of which are undesirable.

Moreover, I feel that the child within us needs to be afraid of violence, only then will the parent in us never use it to discipline our child or prove a point. A peaceful ambience at home works like magic on the tender minds and they grow to become individuals who are fearless in sharing their viewpoint without trepidation.

Relationships are short-lived where one is superior and the other inferior. Bonds live forever when the other is treated as a Co-Equal.

ᚦᚦᚦ

"Children are not things to be moulded, but are people to be unfolded."- Jess Lair

ᗰᗰᗰ

SEVEN
REIMBURSE

Every investment is expected to yield returns. We can say that parenting is an intangible, emotional investment that yields returns in the form of happy and aware individuals. How would it feel to see our children repay our conscious efforts with rude and harsh manners?

ᏢᏢᏢ

In his first year of schooling, my son dressed as an Air Force pilot on 'community helpers' day. When I went to pick him up from school, his teacher signalled me to wait.

"Could you please step aside ma'am? I want to talk to you," she said.

I did as asked and waited as she handed the children over to their parents.

"Ma'am" she started "your son was seen using a bad word in class"

I did not respond as I was shocked.

"There were other boys dressed as policemen in his class. He called one of them 'bloody policeman'. I want to stress that we do not encourage such language and I expect him not to act inappropriately in the future."

I returned holding his hand in mine, still in disbelief that my 3-year-old had spoken those words.

"Did you say something to a boy dressed as a policeman today?" I asked him.

"He was saying he is better than me" he explained

"Where did you pick up bad words from? Did you hear someone use such words at home?" I enquired further, knowing well that we were very careful of our language in his presence.

"I saw that uncle saying that to a policeman in the movie on TV yesterday."

I was not angry anymore. I went back home, shared the incident with my husband, and made sure we were mindful of what we watched on TV when he was around.

I was annoyed at our ignorance but more so was amazed at my son's grasping capacity. We thought he was playing with his toys and paying no attention to what was happening around him. The truth is, despite being engrossed in their activity, children have an unbelievable talent for picking up unwanted and sometimes unacceptable behaviour.

The incident sparked my reflection that if we want them to keep their innocence intact, we must be watchful of the media we consume. The child in us needs to go back to watching non-violent content (at least in the presence of little ones). I'm really fond of animation movies and cartoon and I don't hold back from delighting myself by enjoying them with my son.

❦❦❦

It is a virtue, however, to have children who consider not repaying but reimbursing the lost wishes of their parents.

Recently, a relative of someone I know recently got married. 'So what?' you may think, everyone gets married. It was the second marriage. 'Nothing new' you may say. Many try to change the course of their lives after losing their loved ones. What would you say if I told you that the man who got married was 60 years old??

It was difficult to absorb, startling and unexpected. Every person who heard about this either laughed at the man or spoke ill about this old newly married couple. I was thinking what was wrong with it?

When nobody questions people who get married at 20, 25 or 30, why do it for someone who's 60? Everybody needs and has a right to have a companion. Why was it immoral for a widower living alone to find someone who lives alone like him?

The story goes like this: a lady whose children are married passed away. Her husband, (I'll refer to him as uncle) was left dependent even for a cup of tea. The daughters-in-law would finish their daily chores and head back to their rooms, and the widower was left alone.

The woman (Aunty as I would like to call her) was a widow and had two married sons both settled in the US. The sons wanted to take their mother with them, but she did not want to leave her home, her country.

Hence this marriage came along. The children of both uncle and aunty happily agreed. It would provide them with a companion to talk to, a caretaker if they fall ill and a friend to cry and laugh with.

ϷϷϷ

We need to ask ourselves this – what do we (as children) do for our parents?

They might have stayed hungry for our tummies to be full. They'd have given up on their dreams to fulfil our desires. They may have foregone their necessities to make way for our wishes. Their list can go on and on.

ﮔﮔﮔ

Children are parents' lifetime investments and there are very rare occasions when children get to pay back. We, as children must try our best to put a stop to our parents' sacrifices. We should relieve them of their unending duties and give them opportunities to enjoy their lives, although a happy and peaceful home is all they desire.

We need to spend time with them. Parents of children are also someone's children. It's only fair for us to get together whenever possible and do things they love.

Perhaps watch them relish their favourite foods, dance to their favourite music, go on pilgrimage or hit the theatre to watch a movie. Possibly planning and sending them on that vacation they never took would just prove to be helpful. Whatever their interests are, our mere participation can make a world of difference to them.

In short, we cannot buy their dreams but we might just get close to pushing them towards the experiences they have long aspired.

They have tirelessly supported us, it's our turn to stand by their decisions and prove that we are neither a debt nor a dead investment.

What do we get in return? With a heart filled with oodles of love and happiness, teary eyes and unending smile, they would revert "You think about us, that's all that matters"

ﮔﮔﮔ

I would like to share a personal example here. Just before writing this book, I took up a workshop that required me to be online for two to three hours every day for three consecutive days.

My son would come up to me for something and when he saw that I was attending the workshop, he would go back after whispering "I'll come back later, you finish your workshop"

Even while I'm writing this book, staring at the laptop for hours together, writing, editing and re-editing, he respects the importance of this in my life. When I ask for his suggestions, he puts in great effort to give creative ideas about the cover. I'm so happy that he does not underrate my hobbies or my passion.

For a child his age, he understands that his mother has interests other than the responsibilities of the house. This sensitivity and backing from my little one is the personification of the reimbursement I'm referring to.

It also fortifies my belief that he not only observes how I and my husband behave in the presence of our parents but also organically absorbs it and reflects it in his code of conduct. He considers my choices just like we consider our parents' choices.

ᐅᐅᐅ

Not only that, our way of reciprocating to those who have been of the least help also defines our character. One of my friends from college had once asked me to accompany her for shopping. We went to different shops looking for what she needed and returned empty-handed from all of them.

"I noticed a very unique thing about you today," she said as we walked back. "I noticed that you thanked every shopkeeper as we stepped out."

"I have a habit of doing that. It doesn't matter if we find what we want. If someone has spare time to listen to what we need and look for it, he/she deserves a thank you," I said.

"That's such a priceless thought!" she concluded.

I realized that day that it stood out to her because not many of us practice it.

ᏬᏬᏬ

When my son grew up and was able to speak and ask for something, I would always motivate him to thank me.

"You forgot something," I pointed out every time I noticed him getting what he needed but not reciprocating.

He would meekly blurt a thank you and go ahead.

Thank you is such a small word, yet it holds so much power. It can make someone feel important or add one good thing to someone's terrible day. With the attitude of gratitude, we teach them to value every effort made by someone to make things easier for us, irrespective of whether the person is known to us or a stranger.

ᏬᏬᏬ

I started by thanking him for the small things like passing the napkin, answering the phone, emptying leftovers from his plate before placing it in the sink and even when he lets me have my alone time.

He also watches me as I thank the postman who brings a letter, the vegetable vendor who bills the vegetables, the person at the juice centre who makes us a fresh glass of juice, the auto driver who brings us home, and even the municipality worker taking garbage from our home.

Now I feel happy to see him as he says thank you when he buys candy or ice cream, every time I cook a meal for him, every time his grandmother gives him money to buy chips, and every time his father plays a game of cricket with him.

He also makes sure his younger brother and sister thank him whenever he offers any help to them.

ᚦᚦᚦ

One of Cherith's cousins takes a very disturbing habit from his father. He asks for food, eats it when served and leaves it there for his mother to clear. He has seen his father do the same with his grandmother and he has grown to imbibe the same habit.

"You should clear your plate after eating," he told the boy once.

"Mom is there to do that, why should I?" he replied

"You should, because you have eaten." My son said firmly.

ᚦᚦᚦ

How we behave in the presence of our parents influences them as much as our actions in the presence of our children. Our habits have such a great impact on them. Children who disrespect their parents are likely to be treated the same way by their children when they become parents. Life comes full circle!

A child who values the presence of parents and appreciates all that they do is more likely to be a parent who will be forever grateful to be blessed with a child. This feeling overpowers all the others that stimulate stress, hesitation and self-doubt about our parenting ways. All in all, the good deeds we do for our parents undoubtedly influence our children positively.

ᚦᚦᚦ

"Don't worry that children never listen to you; worry that they are always watching you."- Robert Fulghum

🖤🖤🖤

EIGHT
FOLLOW – ON

A few months back, two very small but big things happened.

My father-in-law's far-off relatives were in town and my husband decided to invite them for breakfast. While telling me more about them, my husband mentioned how my father-in-law was dearly fond of them and that's why he wanted to invite them.

So I prepared 3 South Indian dishes and hoped they had a good meal. They came home, had breakfast and relived a few memories with my father-in-law by telling his children about the times they were together.

After they left, my thoughts drifted to a person whom my mother looked after like a daughter. Impulsively, I picked my phone and dialled her number.

She worked as a house help for my aunt when we stayed in the same building. She may have not worked at our home but never refused to help when my mother called her for help with some extra work or just to meet her and talk to her.

She fondly called my mother - mummy as she had lost her mother when she was a little girl. Her aunt who worked for us got her along many times, hence the acquaintance.

It's still all fresh in my mind, her conversations with Mom, the way she used to look up to her. How she adored her just for being a pure, calming soul in this unjust, cruel world. She would apologize unstoppably whenever mom called her and she couldn't come over and would go back grateful when mom told her "It's okay if you don't come to work, but make sure you come and meet me once in a few days."

When she picked the call, I could sense overwhelming exhilaration in her voice to get a call from me. We exchanged pleasantries and I told her I just thought about her and called.

She told me how mom used to call her to meet every 20-25 days. She fell quiet after saying "I don't get a call frequently from home now but I miss mummy so much..." She could not complete the sentence but I could hear her sobbing.

I told her to go home whenever she could and meet the others in the family. I politely hung up as I found myself at a loss for words to continue. I wondered how Mom managed to talk to her for a longer time.

My father-in-law and my mother are no longer around to guide and bless us but that day, with tears rolling down my cheeks; I realized how we missed out on seeing this side of our parents. They are gone but still remembered and loved.

There are so many people not related to them, but they think about them, miss them, look up to them, talk about them and silently pray they were still around. I asked myself "What would they have done?" and someone from within answered, "They cared!"

ᗡᗡᗡ

They cared for everyone irrespective of their social stature, their distance or even their being close or far-off relatives. This also reminded me of another person who called my mother fortnightly to give updates about what was happening in his life.

It was her distant cousin who never missed meeting her when in Bangalore. He shared his true self with her over the long phone calls. She was the first one he had called after eloping and getting married. I reckon sitting next to her when she picked the telephone and almost shouted. She was so happy and upset at the same time. There are many such people that I can list about my mom and I guess my husband could do the same in my father-in-law's case.

That day, I was somehow very happy and proud of my husband. His effort to grab an opportunity to maintain his father's bond with the people he cared about touched my heart differently.

Making donations and having prayer services for the departed are special undoubtedly but making their special ones feel connected is inexpensively priceless.

ppp

A small gesture or just a phone call is all it takes for us to make a difference in someone's life or even brighten the day for someone. We should not let that chance go.

I and my siblings usually discuss our childhoods when we had very little time with our father and also how our mother never went through our books to check if we had finished our homework. How they never set a bar for us about marks to be obtained, trophies or medals or certificates to win or even the way we should behave.

They did not spend hours running behind us to have a stomach-full meal, teaching us the value of food. They never taught us the value of money. They just did not give it to us unless asked for and sometimes after a lot of requests. They may not have complimented us or thrown parties at our achievements but they took pride in sharing them with others. They may not have celebrated every birthday but they always blessed us and wished for our well-being, good health and success.

�देᏰᏰ

In retrospect, I can say that all of it made us independent. We were responsible for our work as we knew the consequences of not finishing it. We fought and picked at each other but came back together stronger than before every single time. Presently the bond between us is unshakable and unbreakable. We trust each other and perhaps that's the lesson our parents wanted us to learn. To have each other's backs come what may.

ᏰᏰᏰ

With all the new adaptations of playing the new role of a parent, let us be the child that chooses to keep a few good traits of our parents. Let us maintain relationships without being selfish. Let us nurture friendships that do not rely on distances and are not driven by conveniences.

We need to tell our children that we love them. Let us not handhold them at every step. Let us trust their way of doing things and be available when they need us. Let us also prepare them for a world that is different from ours, just like our parents did.

This, in turn, will let our parenting ways have some follow-on from our parents' lifestyle. Despite the challenges and our shortcomings, we will stay afloat if we believe we can do it. That will keep us gratified as children to our parents and be mindful as parents to our children.

ϡϡϡ

"Only children believe they are capable of everything." - Paulo Coelho

ϡϡϡ

NINE
CONCLUSION

"There are no seven wonders of the world in the eyes of a child. There are seven million."- Walt Streightiff

In this racing and pacing world, it is challenging to keep children grounded. In reality, truth, honesty, love, loyalty, compassion, and humility are all felt and nurtured rather than being taught.

While we aim to help our children succeed, we must not suppress their true identities.

Our children are still developing and will learn and grow in due time. We shouldn't stifle their mischief, innocence, or creativity.

We do aim to teach our children to respect elders and women and to refrain from lying and cheating. At the same time, we want them to follow their hearts, make mistakes, fall and have the courage to rise again. When we become a part of the same clan and view things from the same point of view, we can support each other and enrich our bonds.

Let us inculcate the habit of helping. Let's be active players of at least one sport. Let us focus on the value of giving and earning respect. Let's lead a life that promotes healthy eating and honesty. Let our curiosity be our guide.

Let us cherish life's little joys and deal with problems as they appear.

ϸϸϸ

Parenting is an ongoing journey, not a task with a deadline. We are privileged that our children have come to this world through us. We cannot be the ones to decide the course of their lives, forcing choices on them. It is unfair to fulfil our dreams through our child, and to burden them with the baggage of our shortcomings.

We would be making a mistake to believe that our child's success or failure solely rests on our guidance. Their understanding of life, self-confidence, diligence, commitment, and attitude will design the portraits of their life.

We must make ourselves available to listen to our children when they want to talk, empathize when they share secrets, fuel courage when they are failing and celebrate with them in their victories.

Life as a whole is worth a treasure if we put all our experiences together. The best in us comes out when we let go of the stress from the outside world and let our inner child take over. The Key is to take life a little less seriously.

ϸϸϸ

We live to the fullest only when we are carefree. Recall the carefree moments - train journeys we took as children. Travel back to enjoying a popsicle, playing in the streets, singing out of tune, offbeat dancing, drawing and colouring, indulging in cotton candy and bouncing balloons. The little things made us immensely happy.

With our children, we have the opportunity to cherish our golden days and relive them with our little munchkins.

May there be light in all our hearts and may that light guide future generations to a brighter tomorrow.

I am not the perfect parent. I'm just trying to be a child again before striving to become a good parent.

ᡦᡦᡦ

Someone has anonymously yet wisely said *"Children are great imitators. So give them something great to imitate."*

ᡦᡦᡦ

Books By The Author

Nav – Udit (new beginning)

❤❤❤